# Pie Path

Peri just pulled her pie from the oven. Can you help her get it to the pie-baking contest before it cools?

**Answer on page 64**

Start

Finish

1

3

7

44

# Got Space?

Renfru is trying to reach his home planet of Xylo by the time the three suns set on it. Can you help him find his way home? Just one path will lead him there. After you've found the way, write down the letters along the path in order from START to FINISH to answer the question below. Now get zooming!

Answer on page 64

START →

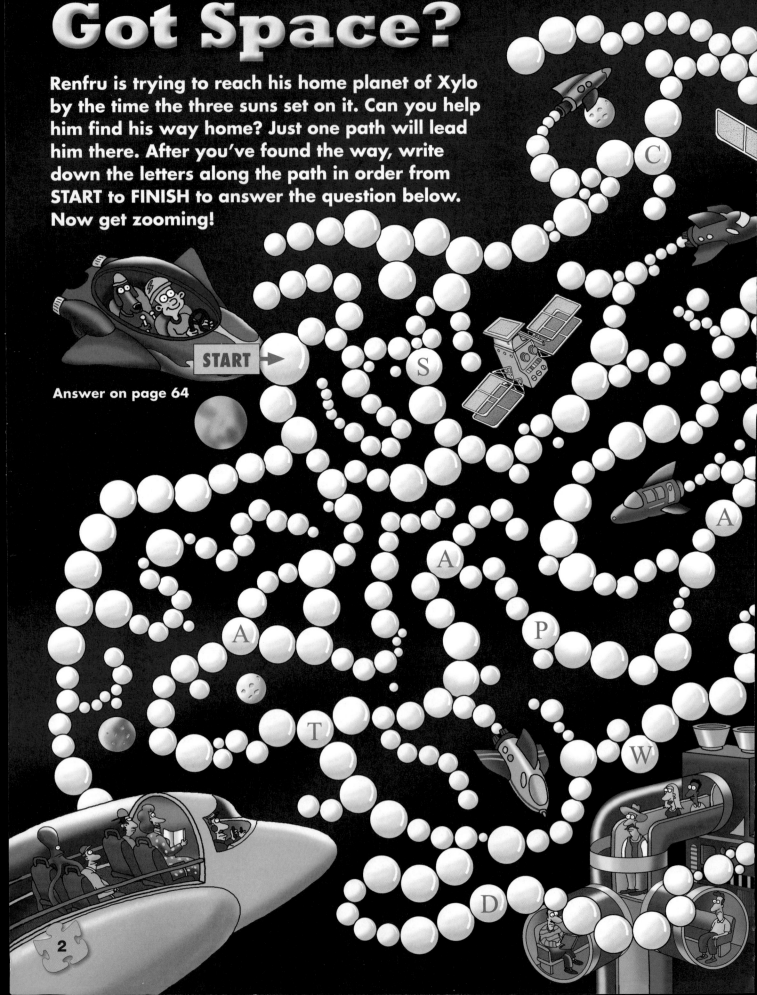

C
S
A
A
P
A
T
W
D

2

**Where will Renfru leave his spaceship when he reaches Xylo?**

ILLUSTRATED BY STEVE SKELTON

3

# Yo No!

Welcome to the **Yo-Yo Olympics**. Things have gotten a little out of hand during the freestyle competition. Follow the strings and see which yo-yo belongs to each person.

**Answer on page 64**

5

# Monkey in the Middle

It's a marvelous day for bananas. Just one of these four paths will take Marty to his treat. Can you help him find the right route? If you do, he'll thank you a whole bunch! When you're done, write the letters you found along the route in order in the spaces below to see the answer to the riddle.

**Answer on page 65**

Finish

**What do you call a flying primate?**

_ _ _ _ _ - _ _ _ _ _ _ _ _

ILLUSTRATED BY STEVE SKELTON

# Jump on In!

The big race is about to start. Follow each frog's path to find out where each happy hopper finishes in the race. Once you've done that, write the letters from the path of the frog who got first place in order in the spaces below. They will spell the answer to the riddle. Now hop to it!

**Answer on page 65**

Hip Hop

Croaker

Zeus

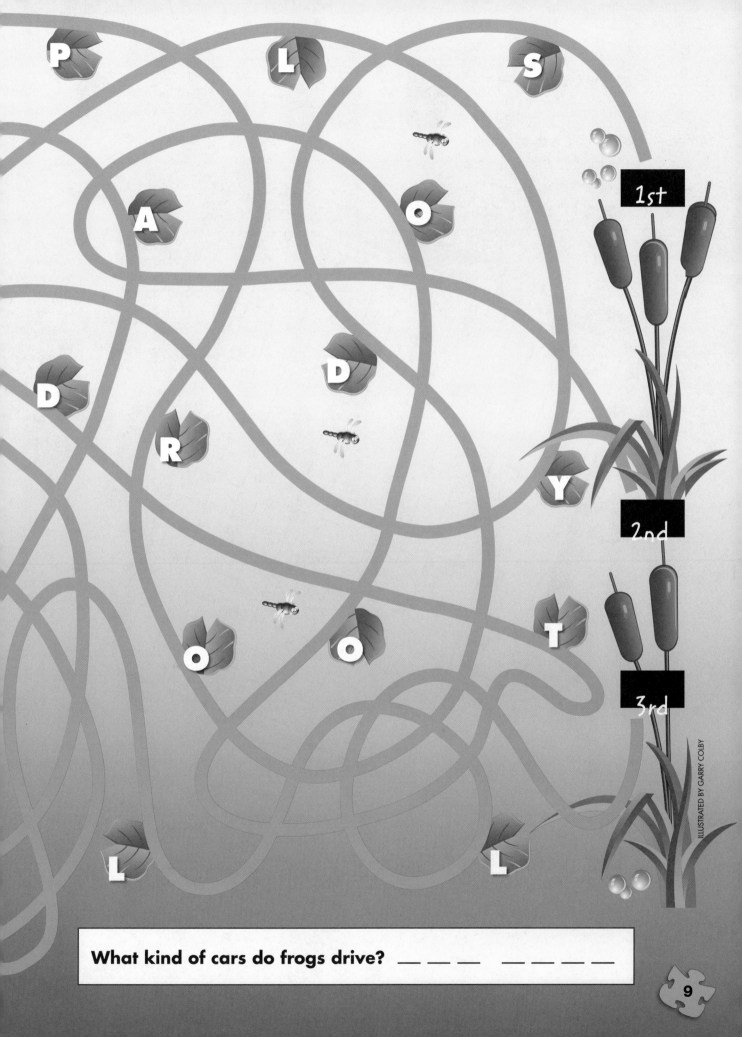

**What kind of cars do frogs drive?** ___ ___ ___   ___ ___ ___ ___

# Letter Drop Drop Drop

Only six of the letters in the top line will work their way through this maze to land in the numbered squares at the bottom. When they get there, they will spell out the answer to the riddle.

**Answer on page 65**

R H A I P R O H C O K O P

1 2 3 4 5 6

What is a rabbit's favorite kind of music?

ILLUSTRATED BY PIXELBOY STUDIO

# The Right Route

It's Groundhog Day, and Phil is late for his big appearance.
Can you help him find the path to the top? Only one route will
take you there. Don't get grounded along the way!

**Answer on page 65**

Finish

FEBRUARY (2)

Start

11

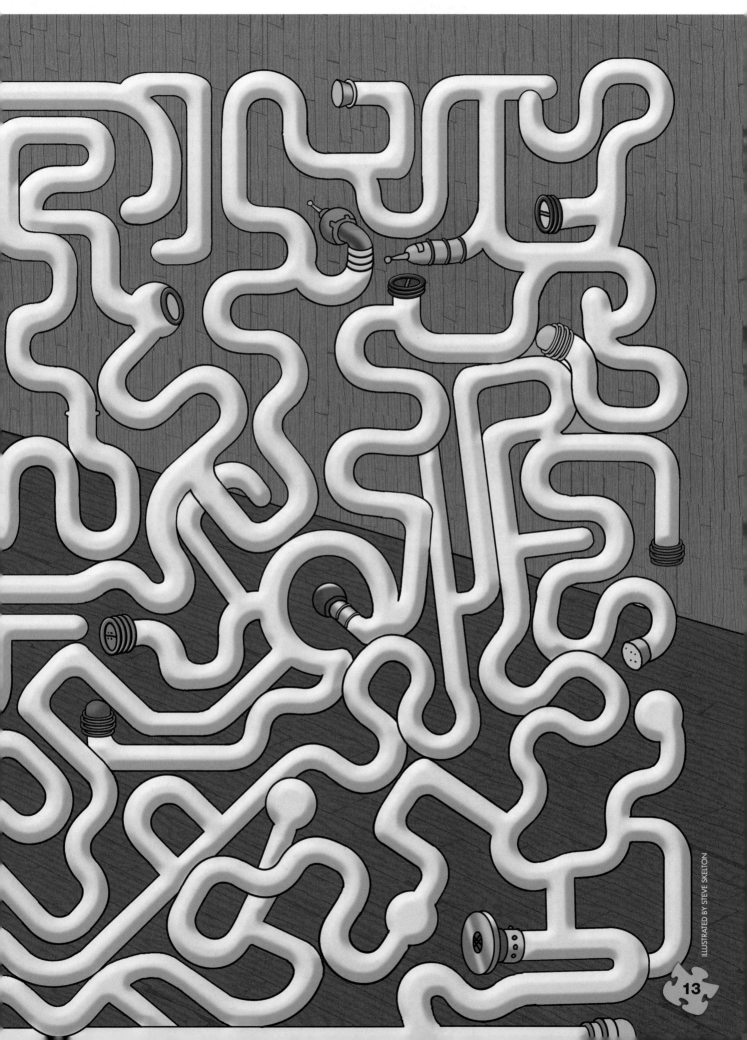

13

# Moonlighting

Trevor and his family took a hike in the moonlight. Now they need help finding the way back to their campsite. Can you find the path that will take them to their tents?

Answer on page 66

Start

Finish

ILLUSTRATED BY PAUL RICHER

14

# Go Cart!

Riley's mom sent her to the store with the world's longest shopping list. Now Riley can hardly see over the groceries in her cart! Can you help her find the right path to the checkout counter?

**Answer on page 66**

Start

Finish

# Uphill Climb

Rocky is almost to the summit of the cliff. Can you help him find his footing the rest of the way? Just one path will take him to the top.

**Answer on page 66**

Finish

Start

# Mind Your Marbles!

Two marbles are about to go on a roll through this marvelous marble maze. Where will the **red** one come out? Where will the **blue** one come out?

**Answer on page 66**

# Rolling on the River

Help Kayak Jack and his faithful dog, Buster, paddle all the way down Rio Splasho. The letters on the correct path will spell the answer to the riddle waiting at the FINISH dock.

**Answer on page 66**

Start

What was
Buster at the end
of his trip?

○○○ ○○○

Finish

19

# Roving Robots

Doodad, Widget, and Whorl have rolled to the corners of this maze. But Glitch is stuck in the middle. Can you help Glitch roll to the empty corner?

Answer on page 67

Start

Finish

# Weight a Second!

Emma weighs 78 pounds. She has to take three one-pound bowling pins across a bridge that will hold only 80 pounds. How can she do it? Follow each line from a letter to a blank space and write the letter in that space. When you are finished, you will have the answer.

**Answer on page 67**

G T E H J M E L U G

G

# Cut It Out!

Gus was cutting the lawn when his mower got away from him. Can you help Gus catch up to his mower? Just one path will take you there.

**Answer on page 67**

Start

R

B

C

C

E

A

A

Y

S

S

R

R

A

22

**Bonus Puzzle**

Once you've found the correct path, write the letters along it in order in the spaces below. They'll answer this riddle:

**What do fishermen plant in their lawns?**

○ ○ ○ ○ ○ ○ ○ ○ ○

23

# Log Jamming

**Grab your wetsuit! This log is about to take the plunge. Can you steer it smoothly all the way to the FINISH without getting soaked? Just one path will take you there.**

Answer on page 67

Start

Finish

# Bull's-Eye

This parachuter is floating to Earth. Can you help him land safely right on target?

Answer on page 67

ILLUSTRATED BY JIM STECK

# In Plane View

These paper airplanes have all come in for a landing, but where?
Follow each path to see where each person's plane ended up.
Enjoy the ride!

**Answer on page 67**

# Ant Eater

Can you help this ant find its way to the food? Just one path will take it there. Try not to get too antsy along the way!

**Answer on page 68**

Finish

Start

ILLUSTRATED BY MATTIA CERATO

# Pencil Paths

Answer on page 68

Which pencil wrote each word?

1

5

2

3

4

29

# Fantastic Gymnastics

It's the day of the big tumbling competition. Can you help Maura with her routine? First, find the one path that goes from START to FINISH. Then use the letters you find along the path to answer the riddle.

Answer on page 68

Start

How do gymnasts feel after a routine?

# Catch This!

*Thwack!* It's a high-fly ball. Will it get over the fence? Follow the path of the ball to see if anyone can make the catch.

Answer on page 68

# Tree Trek

Willow's friends built a brand-new tree house. She can't wait to climb aboard! Can you help Willow find the one path across her neighborhood that will take her there?

**Answer on page 69**

Start

Finish

ILLUSTRATED BY MIKE MORAN

33

# Swim Meet

Kiera wants to meet her friend at the far end of the pool. Can you find the one path that will take her there?

**Answer on page 69**

Start

## Bonus Puzzle

Did you find the path? Now write all the letters you found on it, in order, in the spaces below. They'll answer the riddle.

**Where do minivans go swimming?**

_____ _____ _____ _____ _____ _____ _____

ILLUSTRATED BY RON ZALME

35

# Meet the Beetles

Mingo is meeting up with his friends. They've all made it to the middle of the maze. Can you help Mingo find his way there?

**Answer on page 69**

**Start**

**Finish**

# Movie Maze

Steven is meeting his friends for a movie. But first he has to find the movie theater! Can you help him find the one path that will take him there? Hurry, it's almost showtime!

**Answer on page 69**

Start

Finish

ILLUSTRATED BY MIKE MORAN

# For Fun

Frieda and Freddy are in the house—the fun house! Can you help them find their way through it and back outside? Find the one path that goes from START to FINISH. Have fun!

**Answer on page 70**

Start

ILLUSTRATED BY JIM PAILLOT

Finish

39

# Jump on It!

These jump ropers need to find their partners. Follow each rope to see who is partnered with whom. Go ahead, jump on in!

**Answer on page 70**

40

# Recycle It!

Arun is headed to the recycling center. On the way he has to pick up three bags of things to recycle. Can you help him reach each item and unscramble its name? Once you've got each one, continue along the path until you get to the center. Just one path will take you from **START** to **FINISH**.

Answer on page 70

Start

SNAPPEREW

ILLUSTRATED BY STEVE SKELTON

CLASTIP

ROADDCRAB

Finish

# Sun Spot

This lizard wants to meet up with his friends at their favorite place to lounge in the sun. Can you find the one path that will take him there?

Answer on page 70

Start

O S N K U A D C L M V

# Bonus Puzzle

Did you find the path? Now write all the letters you found on it, in order, in the spaces below. They'll answer the riddle.

**What do lizards wear on their feet?**

_ _ _ _ _ _ _ _ _

# Knit Pick

Follow each person's yarn to see what he or she is knitting.

Answer on page 71

ILLUSTRATED BY JIM PAILLOT

# Crab Walk

This hermit crab needs a new shell. Can you find the path that will take him to his new home?

Answer on page 71

**Start**

**Finish**

# Flip Out!

It's the big disc-golf game. Everyone has just flipped a disc, but whose disc will hit a target? Follow the paths to see where each person's disc lands.

**Answer on page 71**

48

## Bonus Puzzle

Did you find the path? Now write all the letters you found on it, in order, in the spaces below. They'll answer the riddle.

**Where does an amoeba surf?**

___ ___ ___ ___ ___ ___ ___ ___

# It's a Jungle Out There

**Can you help these monkeys find their way to the big concert? Just one path will take them there.**

Answer on page 72

**Start**

52

**Finish**

## Bonus Puzzle

Did you find the path to FINISH? Now write the letters along it, in order, in the spaces below to answer this riddle.

**What do you get if you cross an orchestra with a bunch of monkeys?**

___ ___ ___ ___ ___ - ___ ___ ___ ___ ___

# Slippery Slope

Whee! Bianca is about to head down the slope.
Can you help her ski safely to the bottom?

**Answer on page 72**

**Start**

**Finish**

# Letter Drop

Only six of the letters in the top line will work their way through this maze to land in the numbered squares at the bottom. When they get there, they will spell out the answer to the riddle.

**Answer on page 72**

D I B U L X E R E D O O E

1 2 3 4 5 6

**What does a duck wear when he gets married?**

A __ __ __ __ __ __
   1  2  3  4  5  6

ILLUSTRATED BY BRIAN WHITE

# Super Savers

Uh-oh! These people need help. Luckily, *Puzzlemania*'s four finest superheroes are on the job! But first they need to get there. Can you help them come to the rescue? Follow the paths to take each superhero to where he or she needs to go.

**Answer on page 72**

# Rock It

These rock climbers got their ropes tangled. Can you set them straight? Follow each rope from the climber on the mountain to find out who his or her partner is.

**Answer on page 72**

ILLUSTRATED BY JIM PAILLOT

# Dog Run

Buster wants to meet up with his friends at the dog park. Can you help him sniff out the one trail that will take him there?

**Answer on page 73**

Start

Finish

# Bottled Up

Ella found a bottle washed up on the beach. It has a secret riddle message inside! To find the answer to the riddle, first find the one path from START to FINISH. Then write the letters you find along the way in the spaces below.

**Answer on page 73**

Start

What's the best place to dance at the beach?

ILLUSTRATED BY DAVID COULSON

# Mail Call!

This postal carrier has one last letter to deliver today. Can you help him find the path to the mailbox? When you're done, write the letters along the route in the spaces below to answer the riddle.

**Answer on page 73**

**What is the best kind of letter to read on a hot day?**

_ _ _  _ _ _ _

ILLUSTRATED BY JIM PAILLOT

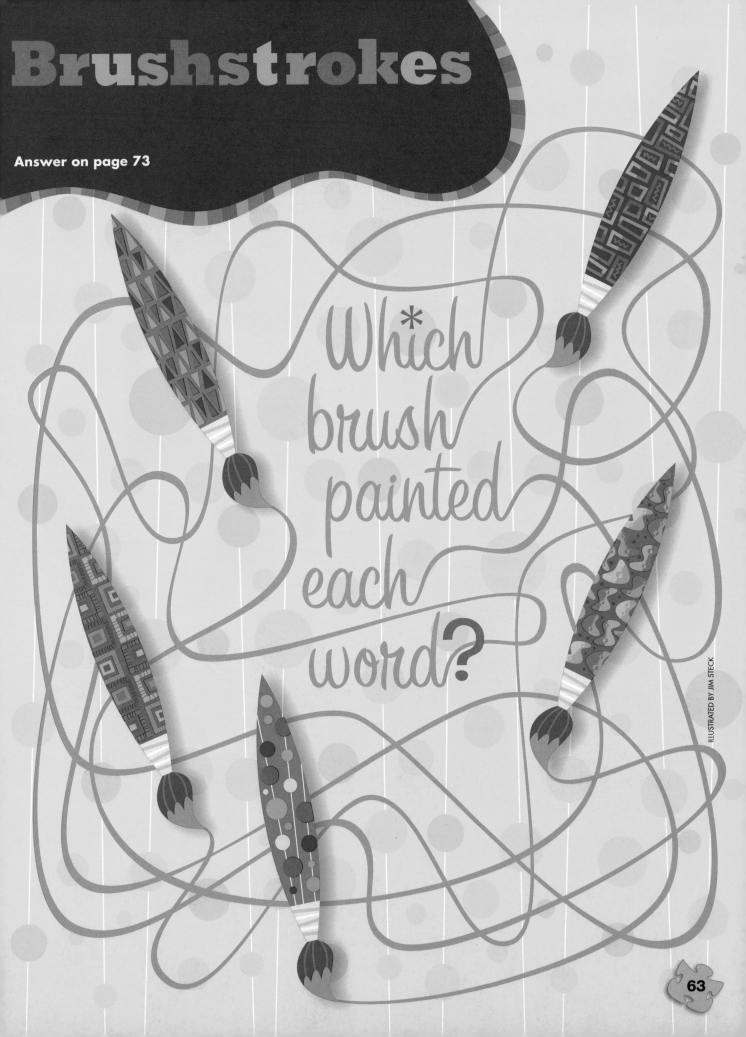

# Answers

Cover

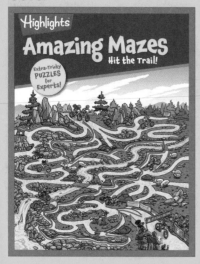

**1** Pie Path

**2–3** Got Space?

Where will Renfru leave his spaceship when he reaches Xylo?

**AT A PARKING METEOR**

**4–5** Yo No!

**6–7** Monkey in the Middle

What do you call a flying primate?

**A HOT-AIR BABOON**

**8–9** Jump on In!

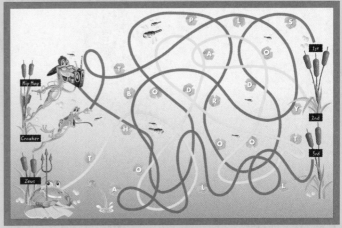

What kind of cars do frogs drive?

**HOP RODS**

**10** Letter Drop

What is a rabbit's favorite kind of music?

**HIP HOP**

**11** The Right Route

**12–13** Lab Labyrinth

# Answers

**14** Moonlighting

**15** Go Cart!

**16** Uphill Climb

**17** Mind Your Marbles!

**18–19** Rolling on the River

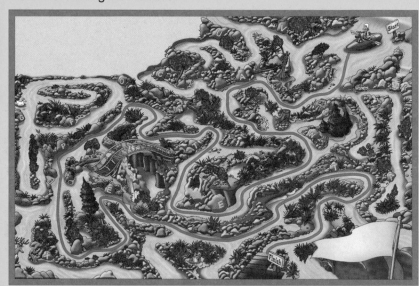

What was Buster at the end of his trip?

**A WET PET**

**20** Roving Robots

**21** Weight a Second!

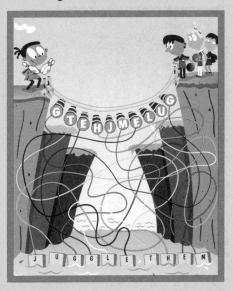

**22–23** Cut It Out!

What do fishermen plant in their lawns? **CRABGRASS**

**24** Log Jamming

**25** Bull's-Eye!

**26–27** In Plane View

# Answers

**28** Ant Eater

**29** Pencil Paths

**30–31** Fantastic Gymnastics

How do gymnasts feel after a routine?
**HEAD OVER HEELS**

**32** Catch This!

**33** Tree Trek

**34–35** Swim Meet

Where do minivans go swimming?
**IN A CARPOOL**

**36** Meet the Beetles

**37** Movie Maze

# Answers

**38–39** For Fun

**40–41** Jump on It!

**42–43** Recycle It!

NEWSPAPER, PLASTIC, CARDBOARD

**44–45** Sun Spot

What do lizards wear on their feet?

**SNAKERS**

70

**46** Knit Pick

**47** Crab Walk

**48–49** Flip Out!

**50–51** Surf to Turf

Where does an amoeba surf?

**ON A MICROWAVE**

# Answers

## 52–53 It's a Jungle Out There

What do you get if you cross an orchestra with a bunch of monkeys?

**A CHIMP-PHONY**

## 54 Slippery Slope

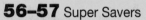

## 55 Letter Drop

What does a duck wear when he gets married?

**A DUXEDO**

## 56–57 Super Savers

## 58 Rock It